Ways Into RE

Places of Worship

Louise Spilsbury

W
FRANKLIN WATTS
LONDON•SYDNEY

Published by Franklin Watts
338 Euston Road
London NW1 3BH

Franklin Watts Australia
Level 17/207 Kent Street
Sydney NSW 2000

ISBN 978 1 4451 3043 9
Dewey classification: 203.5

Series editor: Julia Bird
Art director: Jonathan Hair
Design: Shobha Mucha
Consultant: Joyce Mackley, RE Advisor at RE Today

A CIP catalogue record for this book is available
from the British Library.

Picture credits:
Rolf Adlercreutz/Alamy: 24bl; Ark Religion/Alamy: 11tr, 15t;
Asia/Alamy: 22; Aldar Ayazbayer/istockphoto: 25;
Irdina Borut/istockphoto: 3, 7t; Marshall Bruce/istockphoto: 8b;
Chris Fairclough/Watts Archive: 20; Sally Greenhill/Alamy: 21b;
Richard Gunion/istockphoto: 12tl; Gavin Hellier/Alamy: front cover bl;
Linda Kennedy/Alamy: 26; Art Kowalsky/Alamy: 18b;
Nancy Louie/istockphoto: 10; Neil McAllister/Alamy: 18t;
Holger Mette/istockphoto: 24tr; Jason Moore/Alamy: 16bl;
Erick Ngygen/Alamy: 11cl; Edyta Pawowska/istockphoto: 27;
David Pedre/istockphoto: 7b; Matt Ragen/Shutterstock: 12cr;
Paul Rapson/Alamy: 13; Real Image/Alamy: 6;
Pep Roig/Alamy: 17; Ruby/Alamy: 15b; Linda Steward/istockphoto: 14cl;
Tetra Images/Corbis: front cover br;
Arthur Thévenant/Corbis: 8t; Kheng Guan Toh/Shutterstock: 14r;
Waddell Images/Shutterstock: 16tr; Jim West/Alamy: 23;
World Religions Photo Library: front cover t, 19;
Ron Yue /Alamy: 21t; Zvonkomaja/Shutterstock: 9.

Printed in Malaysia

Franklin Watts is a division of Hachette Children's Books,
an Hachette UK company.
www.hachette.co.uk

Contents

When people worship, they think about and give thanks to their God. People can worship at home or in a special building.

Different religions have different places of worship.

This is a Hindu mandir in Nepal.

Places of worship
Different places of worship have different names.

Buddhist: temples

Hindu: mandirs

Muslim: mosques

Christian: churches

Jewish: synagogues

Sikh: gurdwaras

This tiny church in Greece only has room for a few Christians to worship at a time.

Places of worship for the same religion also look different. Some Christian places of worship are small. Some are huge.

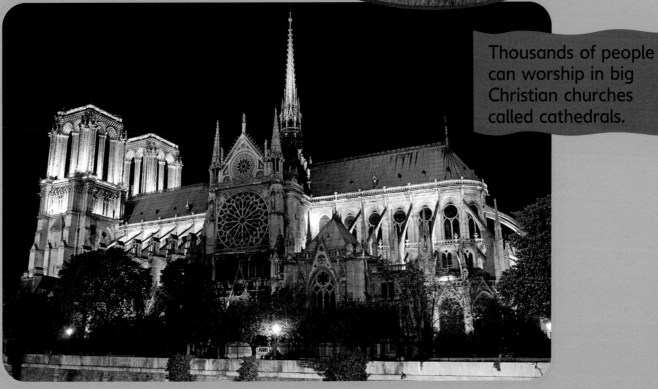

Thousands of people can worship in big Christian churches called cathedrals.

How can you learn about places of worship?
Turn the page to find out.

You can learn a lot about places of worship by looking around outside them.

minaret

dome

Most mosques have round roofs called domes. Next to the dome is a minaret or tower. From here a man calls Muslims to pray.

belltower

A Christian church often has a belltower. Ringing the bells calls people to worship.

How are these places different? How are they similar?

This is a Jewish synagogue. People know it is a synagogue because it is decorated with a Jewish symbol called the Star of David.

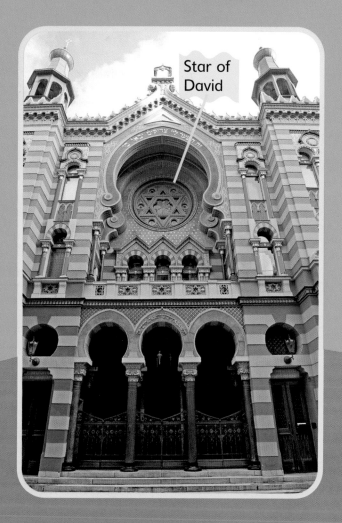

Star of David

Talk about...
...what features tell us what these buildings are from the outside.
Use these words to help you:
- cross
- star and crescent
- Star of David

What do people do before going inside a place of worship?
Turn the page to find out.

Many people prepare themselves before going into their place of worship.

Jewish men and older boys put on a special cap and robes for services in the synagogue.

Why do you think people wear special clothes inside their place of worship?
When do you wear special clothes?

Muslims wash themselves before entering a mosque. This is called wudu.

PLEASE TAKE OFF YOUR
SHOES OUT SIDE THE TEMPLE

Hindus take off their shoes before going inside the mandir.

Talk about...
... how doing special things helps people prepare for worship.
Use these words to help you: •respect •clean •smart •ready •belonging

Places of worship often look, smell and sound special.

Stained glass windows make patterns of coloured light inside some churches.

In temples, mandirs and some churches people burn incense. This perfume smells good and reminds people God is everywhere.

Talk about...

...what you think a place of worship would feel, smell and look like. Use these words to help you:
- peaceful
- quiet
- colourful
- calm
- welcoming
- still

Places of worship may have extra
decoration at special times.
At Christmas, Christians decorate a church with bright
lights and tree branches. People may carry candles.

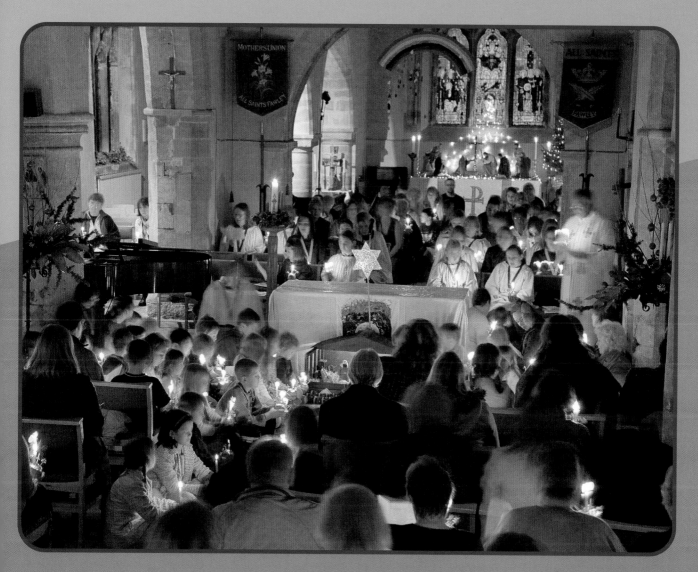

How do you decorate your home for a celebration?
How does this help to make a place special?

Inside places of worship there can be objects that are special to a religion.

The altar is a special table used in church. Some Christians pray and share a little bread and wine at this table to remember God.

In Buddhist temples, there is a statue of Buddha. Buddhists visit the statue and leave gifts as part of their worship.

In synagogues, the Jewish holy books are kept in a cupboard called the Holy Ark. People stand up when these holy books are taken out for readings.

In every gurdwara, there is a throne for the Sikh holy book, the Guru Granth Sahib. People listen to readings from it.

How do you treat precious things?
Do you keep them in a special place?

When people pray, they think about and talk to their God.

To pray in church, people close their eyes and often put their hands together.

In a mosque, people kneel on prayer mats to pray. All Muslims say prayers in the Arabic language.

How do you think being still helps people to pray?

Buddhists do not pray to God. Buddhists say prayers to help them think about what is important.

At the temple, Buddhists turn a prayer wheel. Turning the wheel is meant to repeat the prayer over and over again.

Think about ...

... what people say or ask God when they pray. Use these ideas to help you: •say thank you •ask for something
•say sorry •praise God •ask for help

Places to make music

Singing, playing music and dancing are important parts of worship.

In Hindu mandirs, people sometimes sing hymns. Musicians beat drums and cymbals. People clap their hands.

Christians often sing hymns in church. Hymns are special songs that people sing to give thanks and show love to God.

How do you think the worshippers in these pictures feel?

Taoism is a very old Chinese religion. In a Tao temple, priests and their helpers often lead worship by dancing and playing instruments.

Think about...
... how singing together makes people feel they belong. How does it feel when you sing the same song with other people? How can music say things that may be hard to say using words?

What other things happen in a place of worship? Turn the page to find out.

People learn more about their religion at their place of worship.

In a church, a vicar or minister gives a talk called a sermon from the pulpit.

The sermon teaches people about Jesus and stories from the Bible. The pulpit is high up so everyone can see the speaker.

Some places of worship have schools where children learn about their religion. This is a mosque school.

These children are learning to count in a primary school.

Think about...
... what is the same about the mosque school and the ordinary school. What is different?

Places of worship are also places where people can meet, share meals and talk together.

When Hindu prayers are over, the food that was given as offerings to God becomes holy. Worshippers share and eat the food together.

Why is it important to have somewhere to meet other people of the same religion?

Many places of worship also welcome people from outside their religion.

These Christians are using their church to serve food to homeless people.

Talk about...
...anyone you know who helps people who are in need. How do they help people?

Pilgrimages

Many religions have special places of worship. People go to these places on trips called pilgrimages.

Sikhs visit the Golden Temple of Amritsar. It is made of marble with a layer of gold. It was built by one of the Sikh Gurus.

Many Christians visit Lourdes in France because they believe that water from this place has the power to heal.

All Muslims try to make a pilgrimage to Makkah in Saudi Arabia. Muslims believe Allah was first worshipped here. They pray and worship with millions of other Muslims.

Think about...
... which places are special to you. What do you do there? How do you feel in your special place? Why do people have special places?

How can you learn more about places of worship? Turn the page to find out.

You can find out more about places of worship by visiting some. Before you go, check when you can visit and if there are rules to follow there, such as taking off your shoes or covering your hair.

Think about...

... how to behave when you visit a place of worship.
Use these words to help you:
- respect
- courtesy
- good manners
- politeness

Make a plan about what you would like to find out. Think about questions you would like to ask the people you meet there. What would you ask worshippers, for example?

When you are there, also try to think about how the place feels.

If you cannot visit a real place of worship, use the Internet to explore one.

The world's six main faiths are Hinduism, Christianity, Buddhism, Islam, Judaism and Sikhism. Each of the six main faiths have different beliefs:

Hindus believe there is one God who can take different forms. Hindus worship these different gods and goddesses.

Christians believe there is one God who has three parts: The Father, the Son and the Holy Spirit. Jesus is the son of God and was sent to Earth to save people.

Buddhists do not worship a God. They follow the teachings of a man called Buddha and try to live in the way he taught.

Muslims follow the religion of Islam. They follow five rules known as the Five Pillars: to believe in one God – Allah, to pray five times a day, to fast during the month of Ramadan, to give money to the poor and to go on pilgrimage to Makkah.

Jewish people believe that there is one God who made everything and that they should follow Jewish law.

Sikhs believe that there is one God who made everything. They follow the teachings of ten Gurus (teachers) who told people what God wanted.

Altar – a holy table in a church or temple.

Courtesy – when people are polite and well-behaved towards other people.

Guru – one of the ten important teachers in the Sikh religion.

Holy book – an important book that has teachings or stories about a religion.

Pray – to speak to God.

Pulpit – a high platform where a priest or minister stands so everyone in a church can see and hear them.

Religion – belief in a God or gods. Islam and Christianity are two religions.

Respect – when people behave politely towards something or someone that is important to them.

Sermon – a speech given by a minister or vicar during a church service.

Stained glass – pieces of coloured glass that make church windows.

Statue – a figure of something, such as a person, animal or god, often made from a material such as metal or stone.

Symbol – a picture, word or number that represents something else. A cross is a symbol that represents the Christian Church.

Worship – to show respect or love for God or gods. Some people worship by praying and singing.

Index

About this book

Ways into RE is designed to develop children's knowledge of the world's main religions and to help them respect different religions, beliefs, values and traditions and understand how they influence society and the world. This title, Places of Worship, explores what worship is and what makes places of worship special for people of different religions.

• The children could start by discussing the idea of what worship is and why people may choose to go to special places of worship. If possible, ask children to share experiences and feelings about their own special places, where they can be alone with their thoughts, such as a bedroom or a den. Remind them too that many people also or only worship at home.

• When looking at external features of religious buildings (8–9), you could introduce the idea of symbols by talking about some everyday ones that children will recognise, like the symbol for male and female on a lavatory door or road signs. (Symbols for the different religions are illustrated on page 28.)

• When thinking about the inside of buildings, encourage the children to think about the time and effort that goes into making them special places and how preparing to enter (by washing hands for example) helps people to appreciate the importance of the building and of the worship they go there to do.

• When thinking about places to pray (16–17), the children could talk about how being quiet and still helps people to focus on what is important. In the mosque, a prayer mat shows how a Muslim marks off a special place for being alone.

• If at all possible, arrange a visit to two different places of worship. Children could talk about why it is important to be respectful and quiet on a visit – to show respect and to experience the atmosphere inside. On returning, they could make a class display; draw artefacts or symbols they saw there, with labels explaining meanings; draw a plan of the building; or even role-play a service that they saw there.